EVERYDAY™ CROCHET FOR ALL

17 DESIGNS FOR HOME, APPAREL, & TOYS

If you want your crochet to remain soft while looking new wash after wash, you need Everyday Soft Worsted from the Deborah Norville Collection. This amazing yarn by Premier Yarn is spun with the finest pill-resistant acrylic, making it ideal for projects for the whole family! We asked several of today's popular designers to use Everyday Soft Worsted while creating these accessories. You'll find afghans that thrill you with their color and texture. You can crochet a warm cowl or an innovative scarf set. Make a jacket for your best four-legged friend, and create a cat-nap pillow or a variety of fun toys for a special child. Everyday Soft Worsted comes in 23 rich solid colors and 24 "smart prints" that create the look of stripes or other color-changing patterns without the work. The solids and prints coordinate beautifully with one another, giving you an astonishingly broad palette. Machine washable and dryable, resilient and luxurious, Everyday Soft Worsted is the right yarn for all your crochet needs.

TABLE OF **CONTENTS**

LEISURE ARTS, INC.
Little Rock, Arkansas

COWL SO COZY

EASY

Finished Length: Approx. 12" (30.5 cm)
Finished Circumference: Approx. 43" (109 cm)

MATERIALS

Deborah Norville Everyday™ Soft Worsted Prints (100% acrylic) [3.5 ounces, 180 yards (100 grams, 165 meters) per skein]:
ED200-14 Antique Lavender - 4 skeins
Crochet hook, size N (9 mm) **or** size needed for gauge
Yarn needle

MEDIUM 4

GAUGE: In pattern, (work Flare St, ch 1) 5 times (10 sts) = 4¼" (10.75 cm) and 14 rows/rnds = 6" (15.25 cm)

Gauge Swatch: 5½" wide x 6" high (14 cm x 15.25 cm)
Holding 2 strands of yarn together, ch 15.
Row 1: Hdc in third ch from hook and in each ch across: 13 hdc.
Row 2: Ch 1, turn; sc in first hdc, (ch 1, skip next hdc, sc in next hdc) across: 7 hdc and 6 ch-1 sps.
Row 3: Ch 1, turn; sc in first sc, ch 1, [insert hook in first ch-1 sp and pull up a loop, insert hook in skipped hdc **below** next ch-1 sp and pull up a loop, insert hook in next ch-1 sp (above st just worked in) and pull up a loop, YO and draw through all 4 loops on hook **(first Flare St made)**], ch 1, (work Flare St, ch 1) across to last sc, sc in last sc: 5 Flare Sts, 2 sc, and 6 ch-1 sps.
Row 4: Ch 1, turn; sc in first sc, (ch 1, skip next ch-1 sp, sc in next st) across: 7 hdc and 6 ch-1 sps.
Row 5: Ch 1, turn; sc in first sc, ch 1, [insert hook in first ch-1 sp and pull up a loop, insert hook in skipped ch-1 sp **below** next ch-1 sp and pull up a loop, insert hook in next ch-1 sp (above sp just worked in) and pull up a loop, YO and draw through all 4 loops on hook **(first Flare St made)**], ch 1, (work Flare St, ch 1) across to last sc, sc in last sc: 5 Flare Sts, 2 sc, and 6 ch-1 sps.
Rows 6-14: Repeat Rows 4 and 5, 4 times; then repeat Row 4 once **more**; at end of Row 14, finish off.

STITCH GUIDE

FLARE STITCH *(abbreviated Flare St)*
Insert hook in last ch-1 sp (same sp as last loop of previous st) and pull up a loop, insert hook in skipped st or sp **below** next ch-1 sp and pull up a loop, insert hook in next ch-1 sp (above st or sp just worked in) and pull up a loop, YO and draw through all 4 loops on hook.

Entire Cowl is worked holding two strands of yarn together.

Rnd 1 (Right side)**:** Leaving an 8" (20.5 cm) length for sewing, [ch 3, YO, insert hook in third ch from hook, YO and pull up a loop (3 loops on hook), YO and draw through one loop on hook **(ch made)**, YO and draw through 3 loops on hook **(first fhd made)**], ★ YO, insert hook in ch at base of previous st, YO and pull up a loop (3 loops on hook), YO and draw through one loop on hook **(ch made)**, YO and draw through 3 loops on hook **(fhdc made)**; repeat from ★ 98 times **more**; being careful **not** to twist piece, join with slip st to top of first fhdc: 100 fhdc.

Rnd 2: Ch 1, sc in same st, ch 1, skip next st, (sc in next fhdc, ch 1, skip next fhdc) around; join with slip st to first sc: 50 sc and 50 ch-1 sps.

Rnd 3: Ch 1, [insert hook in last ch-1 sp of rnd just completed and pull up a loop, insert hook in skipped fhdc **below** next ch-1 sp and pull up a loop, insert hook in next ch-1 sp (above st just worked in) and pull up a loop, YO and draw through all 4 loops on hook **(first Flare St made)**], ch 1, (work Flare St, ch 1) around; join with slip st to first Flare St: 50 Flare Sts and 50 ch-1 sps.

Rnd 4: Ch 1, sc in same st, ch 1, skip next ch-1 sp, (sc in next Flare St, ch 1, skip next ch-1 sp) around; join with slip st to first sc.

Rnd 5: Ch 1, [insert hook in last ch-1 sp of rnd just completed and pull up a loop, insert hook in skipped ch-1 sp **below** next ch-1 sp and pull up a loop, insert hook in next ch-1 sp (above sp just worked in) and pull up a loop, YO and draw through all 4 loops on hook **(first Flare St made)**], ch 1, (work Flare St, ch 1) around; join with slip st to first Flare St.

Rnds 6-27: Repeat Rnds 4 and 5, 11 times.

Rnd 28: Ch 1, working **around** same st, sc in st in row **below**, sc in next ch-1 sp, (working **around** next Flare St, sc in st in row **below**, sc in next ch-1 sp) around; join with slip st to first sc, finish off.

Design by Shannon Mullett-Bowlsby.

ON-THE-SPOT **SET**

Finished Measurements

Scarf: Approx. 7" wide x 68" long (18 cm x 172.5 cm)
Mittens: Approx. $3^{3}/_{4}$" wide x 11" long (9.5 cm x 28 cm)
Ear Muffs: Approx. 19" in length (48.5 cm)

MATERIALS

Deborah Norville Everyday™ Soft Worsted Solids (100% acrylic) MEDIUM 4
[4 ounces, 203 yards (114 grams, 185 meters) per skein]:
ED100-12 Black - 3 skeins

Deborah Norville Everyday™ Soft Worsted Prints (100% acrylic) MEDIUM 4
[3.5 ounces, 180 yards (100 grams, 165 meters) per skein]:
ED200-12 Flashback - 3 skeins

Crochet hook, size G (4 mm) **or** size needed for gauge
Yarn needle
Polyester stuffing

GAUGE SWATCH: 5" (12.75 cm) diameter
Work Rnds 1-6 of Scarf Circle; do **not** finish off.

SCARF

CIRCLE (Make 10)

With Flashback, ch 4; join with slip st to form a ring.

Rnd 1 (Right side)**:** Ch 1, 6 sc in ring; join with slip st to first sc.

Note: Loop a short piece of yarn around any stitch to mark Rnd 1 as **right** side.

Rnd 2: Ch 3 **(counts as first dc, now and throughout)**, dc in same st, 2 dc in next sc and in each sc around; join with slip st to first dc: 12 dc.

Rnd 3: Ch 1, 2 sc in same st and in each dc around; join with slip st to first sc, finish off: 24 sc.

Rnd 4: With **right** side facing, join Black with slip st in same st as joining; ch 3, dc in same st and in next sc, (2 dc in next sc, dc in next sc) around; join with slip st to first dc: 36 dc.

Rnd 5: Ch 1, sc in same st and in each dc around; join with slip st to first sc, finish off.

Rnd 6: With **right** side facing, join Flashback with slip st in same st as joining; ch 3, dc in same st and in next sc, (2 dc in next sc, dc in next sc) around; join with slip st to first dc: 54 dc.

Rnd 7: Ch 1, sc in same st and in each dc around; join with slip st to first sc, finish off.

Rnd 8: With **right** side facing, join Black with slip st in same st as joining; ch 3, dc in same st, 2 dc in each of next 2 sc, dc in next sc, (2 dc in next sc, dc in next sc) around; join with slip st to first dc, finish off: 82 dc.

ASSEMBLY

Place 2 Circles with **wrong** sides together. With Black and working through **both** loops of **both** pieces, whipstitch 10 sts together *(Fig. 6, page 40)*.

Place next Circle with **wrong** side against **wrong** side of last Circle joined; skip next 31 dc on last Circle joined. With Black and working through **both** loops of **both** pieces, whipstitch next 10 sts together.

Repeat with remaining 7 Circles.

BORDER

To treble crochet (abbreviated tr), YO twice, insert hook in st indicated, YO and pull up a loop (4 loops on hook), (YO and draw through 2 loops on hook) 3 times.

With **right** side facing, join Black with sc in center dc at bottom of end Circle *(see Joining With Sc, page 39)*; ★ sc in each dc around to within 3 dc of seam, hdc in next dc, dc in next dc, tr in next dc, tr in seam and in next dc on **next** Circle, dc in next dc, hdc in next dc; repeat from ★ around, sc in each dc around; join with slip st in first sc, finish off.

MITTEN (Make 2)

HAND

With Black, ch 4; join with slip st to form a ring.

Rnd 1 (Right side)**:** 6 Sc in ring; do **not** join, place marker *(see Markers, page 39)*: 6 sc.

Note: Mark Rnd 1 as **right** side.

Rnds 2 and 3: 2 Sc in each sc around: 24 sc.

Rnd 4: Sc in each sc around.

Rnd 5: (Sc in next 3 sc, 2 sc in next sc) around: 30 sc.

Rnds 6-21: Sc in each sc around.

Rnd 22 (Thumb Opening)**:** Ch 8, skip next 4 sc, sc in next sc and in each sc around: 26 sc and 8 chs.

Rnd 23: Sc in each ch and in each sc around: 34 sc.

Rnds 24 and 25: Sc in each sc around.

Rnd 26: (Sc in next 5 sc, skip next sc) 5 times, sc in next 4 sc: 29 sc.

Rnds 27-30: Sc in each sc around; at end of Rnd 30, slip st in next sc and finish off leaving a long end for sewing.

THUMB

Rnd 1: With **right** side facing and working in free loops of ch-8 *(Fig. 2b, page 39)*, join Flashback with sc in first ch; sc in next 7 chs, sc in each skipped sc on Rnd 21 of Hand; do **not** join, place marker: 12 sc.

Rnds 2-8: Sc in each sc around.

Rnd 9: (Skip next sc, sc in next 2 sc) around: 8 sc.

Rnd 10: Sc in each sc around; slip st in next sc and finish off leaving a long end for sewing.

Thread yarn needle with long end and weave through sc on Rnd 10; gather **tightly** to close and secure end.

CUFF

With Black, ch 17.

Row 1 (Right side)**:** Sc in second ch from hook and in each ch across changing to Flashback in last sc *(Fig. 3a, page 39)*; cut Black: 16 sc.

Row 2: Ch 1, turn; sc in both loops of first sc, sc in Back Loop Only of each sc across to last sc *(Fig. 1, page 39)*, sc in both loops of last sc changing to Black; cut Flashback.

Instructions continued on page 9.

CANINE **COMFORT** EASY

Sizes: Small{Medium-Large-XLarge}
Fits Chest Measurement:
12{16-20-24}"/30.5{40.5-51-61} cm
Finished Body Length:
Approx. 9{10-14-18}"/23{25.5-35.5-45.5} cm

Size Note: Instructions are written for size Small, with sizes Medium, Large, and XLarge in braces { }. Instructions will be easier to read if you circle all the numbers pertaining to your size. If only one number is given, it applies to all sizes.

MATERIALS

Deborah Norville Everyday™
Soft Worsted Prints (100% acrylic) MEDIUM 4
[3.5 ounces, 180 yards
(100 grams, 165 meters) per skein]:
ED200-07 Cold Mountain - 1{1-2-3} skein(s)
Deborah Norville Everyday™
Soft Worsted Solids (100% acrylic) MEDIUM 4
[4 ounces, 203 yards (114 grams, 185 meters) per skein]:
ED100-10 Aubergine - 1 skein
Crochet hook, size G (4 mm) **or** size needed for gauge
3/4" (19 mm) Buttons - 6
Yarn needle
Sewing needle and matching thread

GAUGE: In Body pattern, 14 sts and 14 rows = 4" (10 cm)
Pocket Square Rnds 1 and 2 = 2 1/2" (6.25 cm);
Rnds 1-3 = 3 1/2" (9 cm);
and Rnds 1-4 = 4 1/2" (11.5 cm)

Gauge Swatch: 4 1/4" wide x 4" high (10.75 cm x 10 cm)
Row 1 (Right side)**:** Ch 16; sc in second ch from hook and in each ch across: 15 sc.
Row 2: Ch 1, turn; sc in first sc, ★ dc in next sc, sc in next sc; repeat from ★ across.
Row 3: Ch 1, turn; sc in each st across.
Rows 4-14: Repeat Rows 2 and 3, 5 times; then repeat Row 2 once **more**; at end of Row 14, finish off.

BODY

With Cold Mountain and beginning at tail, ch 18{22-28-40}.

Row 1 (Right side)**:** Sc in second ch from hook and in each ch across: 17{21-27-39} sc.

Note: Loop a short piece of yarn around any stitch to mark Row 1 as **right** side.

Row 2: Ch 1, turn; sc in first sc, ★ dc in next sc, sc in next sc; repeat from ★ across.

Row 3 (Increase row)**:** Ch 1, turn; 2 sc in first sc, sc in each st across to last sc, 2 sc in last sc: 19{23-29-41} sc.

Rows 4 thru 8{12-14-16}: Repeat Rows 2 and 3, 2{4-5-6} times; then repeat Row 2 once **more**: 23{31-39-53} sc.

Row 9{13-15-17}: Ch 1, turn; sc in each st across.

Row 10{14-16-18}: Ch 1, turn; sc in first sc, ★ dc in next sc, sc in next sc; repeat from ★ across.

Rows 11{15-17-19} thru 16{24-32-36}: Repeat Rows 9{13-15-17} and 10{14-16-18}, 3{5-8-9} times.

Row 17{25-33-37}: Turn; slip st in first 2{4-4-4} sts, ch 1, sc in next st and in each st across to last 2{4-4-4} sts, leave remaining 2{4-4-4} sts unworked: 19{23-31-45} sc.

Row 18{26-34-38}: Ch 1, turn; sc in first sc, ★ dc in next sc, sc in next sc; repeat from ★ across.

Row 19{27-35-39} (Decrease row)**:** Ch 1, turn; skip first sc, sc in next st and in each st across to last 2 sts, skip next dc, sc in last sc: 17{21-29-43} sc.

Rows 20{28-36-40} thru 21{31-39-45}: Repeat Rows 18{26-34-38} and 19{27-35-39}, 1{2-2-3} time(s): 15{17-25-37} sc.

Rows 22{32-40-46} thru 26{36-46-52}: Repeat Row 10{14-16-18} once; then repeat Rows 9{13-15-17} and 10{14-16-18}, 2{2-3-3} times; at end of last row, finish off.

BORDER

With **right** side facing and working in free loops of beginning ch *(Fig. 2b, page 39)*, join Aubergine with slip st in center ch; ch 3 **(counts as first dc, now and throughout)**, dc evenly around Body to corner of Row 16{24-32-36}, place marker in last dc made for Chest Band placement, hdc evenly around to opposite end of Row 16{24-32-36}, dc evenly around; join with slip st to first dc, finish off.

POCKET SQUARE

With Aubergine, ch 4; join with slip st to form a ring.

Rnd 1 (Right side): Ch 5 **(counts as first dc plus ch 2, now and throughout)**, (3 dc in ring, ch 2) 3 times, 2 dc in ring; join with slip st to first dc: 12 dc and 4 ch-2 sps.

Note: Mark Rnd 1 as **right** side.

Rnd 2: (Slip st, ch 5, 3 dc) in next ch-2 sp, ch 1, ★ (3 dc, ch 2, 3 dc) in next ch-2 sp, ch 1; repeat from ★ 2 times **more**, 2 dc in same sp as first dc; join with slip st to first dc: 24 dc and 8 sps.

Rnd 3: (Slip st, ch 5, 3 dc) in next corner ch-2 sp, ch 1, 3 dc in next ch-1 sp, ch 1, ★ (3 dc, ch 2, 3 dc) in next corner ch-2 sp, ch 1, 3 dc in next ch-1 sp, ch 1; repeat from ★ 2 times **more**, 2 dc in same corner sp as first dc; join with slip st to first dc: 36 dc and 12 sps.

Rnd 4: (Slip st, ch 5, 3 dc) in next corner ch-2 sp, ch 1, (3 dc in next ch-1 sp, ch 1) twice, ★ (3 dc, ch 2, 3 dc) in next corner ch-2 sp, ch 1, (3 dc in next ch-1 sp, ch 1) twice; repeat from ★ 2 times **more**, 2 dc in same corner sp as first dc; join with slip st to first dc: 48 dc and 16 sps.

Sizes Small and Medium ONLY: Finish off.

Sizes Large and XLarge ONLY - Rnd 5: (Slip st, ch 5, 3 dc) in next corner ch-2 sp, ch 1, (3 dc in next ch-1 sp, ch 1) 3 times, ★ (3 dc, ch 2, 3 dc) in next corner ch-2 sp, ch 1, (3 dc in next ch-1 sp, ch 1) 3 times; repeat from ★ 2 times **more**, 2 dc in same corner sp as first dc; join with slip st to first dc, finish off: 60 dc and 20 sps.

Instructions continued on page 8.

CANINE COMFORT

Continued from page 7.

NECK BAND

Make 5{6-5-6} Squares as follows:
With Cold Mountain, work same as Pocket Square through Rnd 2{2-3-3}; finish off.

With **wrong** sides together, beginning in second ch of first corner and ending in first ch of next corner, and working through **both** loops of **both** pieces, whipstitch Squares together forming a strip ***(Fig. 6, page 40)***.

EDGING

With **right** side facing, join Aubergine with slip st in any corner ch-2 sp; ch 2, hdc evenly around entire strip; join with slip st to top of beginning ch-2, finish off.

With **wrong** sides together and matching top edge (last row) of Body with long edge of Neck Band, whipstitch Body to Neck Band, having excess Neck Band length on left side.

CHEST BAND

Make 2 Squares as follows:
With Cold Mountain, work same as Pocket Square through Rnd 2{2-3-3}; finish off.

Last Rnd: With **right** side facing, join Aubergine with slip st in any corner ch-2 sp; ch 5, 3 dc in same sp, ch 1, (3 dc in next ch-1 sp, ch 1) across to next corner ch-2 sp, ★ (3 dc, ch 2, 3 dc) in corner ch-2 sp, ch 1, (3 dc in next ch-1 sp, ch 1) across to next corner ch-2 sp; repeat from ★ 2 times **more**, 2 dc in same corner sp as first dc; join with slip st to first dc, finish off.

With **wrong** sides together, beginning in second ch of first corner and ending in first ch of next corner, and working through **both** loops of **both** pieces, whipstitch Squares together.

With **wrong** sides together and working through **both** loops of **both** pieces, sew end of Chest Band to Body beginning at marked st.

POCKET FLAP

With Cold Mountain, ch 4; join with slip st to form a ring.

Row 1: Ch 3, (2 dc, ch 2, 3 dc) in ring: 6 dc and one ch-2 sp.

Note: Mark Row 1 of sizes Large and XLarge as **right** side.

Row 2: Ch 3, turn; dc in next 2 dc, (3 dc, ch 2, 3 dc) in next ch-2 sp, dc in last 3 dc: 12 dc.

Note: Mark Row 2 of sizes Small and Medium as **right** side.

Sizes Small and Medium ONLY
Row 3: Ch 3, turn; dc in next 5 dc, (3 dc, ch 2, 3 dc) in next ch-2 sp, dc in next 6 dc changing to Aubergine in last dc ***(Fig. 3b, page 39)***: 18 dc.

Edging: Ch 3, turn; dc in next dc and in each dc across to next ch-2 sp, (3 dc, ch 2, 3 dc) in ch-2 sp, dc in each dc across; working in end of rows, dc evenly across; join with slip st to first dc, finish off.

Sizes Large and XLarge ONLY
Row 3: Ch 3, turn; dc in next 5 dc, (3 dc, ch 2, 3 dc) in next ch-2 sp, dc in next 6 dc: 18 dc.

Row 4: Ch 3, turn; dc in next 8 dc, (3 dc, ch 2, 3 dc) in next ch-2 sp, dc in next 9 dc changing to Aubergine in last dc ***(Fig. 3b, page 39)***: 24 dc.

Edging: Ch 3, turn; dc in next dc and in each dc across to next ch-2 sp, (3 dc, ch 2, 3 dc) in ch-2 sp, dc in each dc across; working in end of rows, dc evenly across; join with slip st to first dc, finish off.

FINISHING

Using photo, page 7, as a guide for placement:
Sew Pocket Square to the Body. Sew Pocket Flap 1/2" (12 mm) above the top of the Pocket. Sew one button to the pocket, opposite the ch-2 sp on Row 3{3-4-4} of Pocket Flap.

Sew 3 buttons to Square at right edge of Neck Band, with one button at center of right edge and remaining 2 buttons at left corners of first Square. Use ch-sps in Square at left end of Neck Band as buttonholes.

Sew 2 buttons to the left side of Body. Use corner ch-2 sps on last rnd of Chest Band Square as buttonholes.

Design by Sharon Mann.

ON-THE-SPOT SET

Continued from page 5.

Row 3: Ch 1, turn; sc in both loops of first sc, sc in Back Loop Only of each sc across to last sc, sc in both loops of last sc changing to Flashback; cut Black.

Rows 4-26: Repeat Rows 2 and 3, 11 times; then repeat Row 2 once **more**, at end of Row 26, do **not** change colors; finish off leaving a 10" (25.5 cm) end for sewing.

With **wrong** sides together and matching sts on Row 26 with free loops of beginning ch, sew Cuff seam.

CIRCLE

With Black, ch 4; join with slip st to form a ring.

Rnd 1 (Right side)**:** Ch 1, 6 sc in ring; join with slip st to first sc.

Note: Mark Rnd 1 as **right** side.

Rnd 2: Ch 3, dc in same st, 2 dc in next sc and in each sc around; join with slip st to first dc, finish off: 12 dc.

Rnd 3: With **right** side facing, join Flashback with slip st in same st as joining; ch 3, dc in same st, 2 dc in next dc and in each dc around; join with slip st to first dc, finish off leaving a long end for sewing: 24 dc.

FINISHING

Sew Cuff to Hand.

Right Mitten: Flatten one Mitten so that the Thumb is at the bottom left. Working in Back Loops Only, sew Circle to the top of Hand.

Left Mitten: Flatten second Mitten so that the Thumb is at the bottom right. Working in Back Loops Only, sew Circle to the top of Hand.

EAR MUFFS

EAR MUFF CIRCLE (Make 2)

Work same as Scarf Circle, page 4, through Rnd 3: 24 sc.

Rnd 4: With **right** side facing, join Black with slip st in same st as joining; ch 3, dc in same st and in next sc, (2 dc in next sc, dc in next sc) around; join with slip st to first dc, finish off: 36 dc.

Rnd 5: With **right** side facing, join Flashback with sc in same st as joining; sc in each dc around; join with slip st to first sc, finish off leaving a long end for sewing.

HEAD BAND

With Black, ch 53.

Row 1: Sc in second ch from hook and in each ch across: 52 sc.

Row 2: Ch 3, turn; dc in next sc and in each sc across changing to Flashback in last dc ***(Fig. 3b, page 39)***; cut Black.

Row 3: Ch 1, turn; sc in each dc across changing to Black in last sc; cut Flashback.

Row 4: Ch 3, turn; dc in next sc and in each sc across.

Row 5: Ch 1, turn; sc in each dc across; finish off.

HEAD BAND CIRCLE

With Flashback, ch 4; join with slip st to form a ring.

Rnd 1 (Right side)**:** Ch 3, 11 dc in ring; join with slip st to first dc: 12 dc.

Rnd 2: Ch 1, 2 sc in same st and in each dc around; join with slip st to first sc, finish off: 24 sc.

TIES (Make 2)

Holding one strand of each color together, chain a 15" (38 cm) length; finish off.

FINISHING

With **wrong** sides together and using long end, whipstitch 2 Ear Muff Circles together working through **both** loops of **both** pieces, stuffing lightly before closing.

Repeat with 2 additional Ear Muff Circles.

Sew ends of Head Band to each stuffed Ear Muff Circle, adjusting so that stuffed Circles fit over ears. Sew Tie to same side of each stuffed Circle as Head Band.

Working in Back Loops Only, sew the Head Band Circle to the center of the Head Band.

Sew remaining 2 Ear Muff Circles to the back of each stuffed Circle to cover end of Head Band and Tie.

Designs by Sharon Mann.

OFFSET RIPPLES

EASY

Finished Measurement:

Approx. 48" x 51" (122 cm x 129.5 cm)

MATERIALS

Deborah Norville Everyday™ Soft Worsted Solids (100% acrylic) MEDIUM 4
[4 ounces, 203 yards (114 grams, 185 meters) per skein]:
- ED100-08 Pine Green - 5 skeins
- ED100-11 Chocolate - 4 skeins

Deborah Norville Everyday™ Soft Worsted Prints (100% acrylic) MEDIUM 4
[3.5 ounces, 180 yards (100 grams, 165 meters) per skein]:
- ED200-16 Oak Moss - 3 skeins

Crochet hook, size I (5.5 mm) **or** size needed for gauge
Yarn needle

GAUGE: Wide Strip = $6^{1}/_{4}$" wide (16 cm)

Gauge Swatch: $4^{1}/_{2}$" wide x 4" long (11.5 cm x 10 cm)
Work same as Narrow Strip for 9 rows.

STITCH GUIDE

DECREASE
Pull up a loop in each of next 2 chs or sc, YO and draw through all 3 loops on hook **(counts as one sc)**.

All stitches are worked in Back Loops Only *(Fig. 1, page 39)*.

NARROW STRIP (Make 4)

Each strip has a total of 117 rows. The stripe sequence in the strips is random and can be changed at your discretion. Simply repeat Row 2 as many times as desired, then work the Transition Row to transpose the colors within your strip.

In the photographed afghan, the Narrow Strips were worked as follows:

FIRST STRIP
Colors used: Pine Green and Chocolate.
Transition Rows: 8, 15, 33, 39, 45, 63, 69, 75, 87, and 105.

SECOND STRIP
Colors used: Chocolate and Oak Moss.
Transition Rows: 16, 32, 42, 54, 65, 75, 85, 97, and 108.

THIRD STRIP
Colors used: Pine Green and Oak Moss.
Transition Rows: 7, 19, 31, 40, 56, 67, 81, 97, and 107.

FOURTH STRIP
Colors used: Pine Green and Chocolate.
Transition Rows: 11, 23, 37, 49, 59, 71, 81, 95, and 105.

Using first color, ch 10; with second color, ch 11.

Row 1 (Right side)**:** Skip first ch from hook, decrease, sc in next 7 chs, 2 sc in next ch changing to first color in last sc made *(Fig. 3a, page 39)*, drop yarn to **wrong** side, 2 sc in next ch, sc in next 7 chs, decrease: 20 sc.

Note: Loop a short piece of yarn around any stitch to mark Row 1 as **right** side.

Row 2: Ch 1, turn; working in Back Loops Only *(Fig. 1, page 39)*, decrease beginning in first sc, sc in next 7 sc, 2 sc in next sc changing to next color in last sc made, drop yarn to **wrong** side, 2 sc in next sc, sc in next 7 sc, decrease.

Repeat Row 2 as many times as desired.

Transition Row: Ch 1, turn; using same color across entire row, decrease beginning in first sc, sc in next 7 sc, 2 sc in each of next 2 sc, sc in next 7 sc, decrease.

At the end of Row 117, finish off.

WIDE STRIP (Make 5)

Each strip has a total of 117 rows. The stripe sequence in the strips is random and can be changed at your discretion. Simply repeat Row 2 as many times as desired, then work the Transition Row to transpose the colors within your strip.

In the photographed afghan, the Wide Strips were worked as follows:

FIRST STRIP
Colors used: Pine Green and Oak Moss.
Transition Rows: 8, 21, 35, 41, 51, 63, 74, 83, 100, 103, and 114.

SECOND STRIP
Colors used: Chocolate and Pine Green.
Transition Rows: 10, 22, 32, 44, 56, 67, 79, 90, 103, and 114.

THIRD STRIP
Colors used: Pine Green and Chocolate.
Transition Rows: 7, 25, 37, 43, 55, 73, 78, 84, 89, and 101.

FOURTH STRIP
Colors used: Pine Green and Chocolate.
Transition Rows: 11, 23, 34, 46, 51, 62, 68, 85, 91, and 101.

FIFTH STRIP
Colors used: Chocolate and Oak Moss.
Transition Rows: 19, 25, 31, 49, 59, 72, 78, 92, and 104.

Using first color, ch 15; with second color, ch 16.

Row 1 (Right side)**:** Skip first ch from hook, decrease, sc in next 12 chs, 2 sc in next ch changing to first color in last sc made, drop yarn to **wrong** side, 2 sc in next ch, sc in next 12 chs, decrease: 30 sc.

Note: Mark Row 1 as **right** side.

Row 2: Ch 1, turn; working in Back Loops Only, decrease beginning in first sc, sc in next 12 sc, 2 sc in next ch changing to next color in last sc made, drop yarn to **wrong** side, 2 sc in next sc, sc in next 12 sc, decrease.

Repeat Row 2 as many times as desired.

Transition Row: Ch 1, turn; using same color across entire row, decrease beginning in first sc, sc in next 12 sc, 2 sc in each of next 2 sc, sc in next 12 sc, decrease.

At the end of Row 117, finish off.

ASSEMBLY

Lay out Strips with beginning chs at same end and alternating Wide and Narrow Strips.

Holding 2 Strips with **wrong** sides together, end of rows matching, and working through **both** thicknesses, join Oak Moss with sc in first row ***(see Joining With Sc, page 39)***; sc evenly across end of rows; finish off.

Repeat with remaining Strips.

With **right** side facing and working in end of rows across long edge, join Oak Moss with sc in end of first row; sc evenly across; finish off. Repeat across second long side edge.

Design by Kim Kotary. ●

CASUAL **COMFORT** EASY

Finished Measurement: Approx. 50" (127 cm) square

MATERIALS

Deborah Norville Everyday™ Soft Worsted Prints (100% acrylic) MEDIUM 4
[3.5 ounces, 180 yards (100 grams, 165 meters) per skein]:
ED200-02 Mint Chocolate Chip - 12 skeins
Crochet hook, size I (5.5 mm) **or** size needed for gauge

GAUGE: In pattern, 17 sts and 12 rows = 5" (12.75 cm)

Gauge Swatch: 5" wide x 4" high (12.75 cm x 10 cm)
Row 1: Work 17 fsc.
Row 2: Ch 1, turn; sc in Front Loop Only of each fsc across *(Fig. 1, page 39)*: 17 sc.
Rows 3-10: Repeat Rows 3 and 4 of Afghan, 4 times.
Finish off.

STITCH GUIDE

FOUNDATION SINGLE CROCHET *(abbreviated fsc)*
Ch 2, insert hook in second ch from hook, YO and pull up a loop, YO and draw through one loop on hook **(ch made)**, YO and draw through both loops on hook **(first fsc made)**, ★ insert hook in ch at base of last fsc made, YO and pull up a loop, YO and draw through one loop on hook **(ch made)**, YO and draw through both loops on hook **(fsc made)**; repeat from ★ for each additional st.

BEGINNING LINKED DOUBLE CROCHET *(abbreviated Beginning Ldc)*
Ch 3, turn; insert hook in second ch from hook, YO and pull up a loop, skip next ch, insert hook in Front Loop Only of first sc, YO and pull up a loop (3 loops on hook), (YO and draw through 2 loops on hook) twice **(beginning Ldc made)**.

LINKED DOUBLE CROCHET *(abbreviated Ldc)*
Insert hook in horizontal bar in the center of the post of the last Ldc made, YO and pull up a loop, insert hook in Front Loop Only of next sc, YO and pull up a loop (3 loops on hook), (YO and draw through 2 loops on hook) twice **(Ldc made)**.

AFGHAN

Row 1: Work 170 fsc.

Row 2 (Right side)**:** Ch 1, turn; sc in Front Loop Only of each fsc across *(Fig. 1, page 39)*: 170 sc.

Note: Loop a short piece of yarn around any stitch to mark Row 2 as **right** side.

Row 3: Work beginning Ldc, work Ldc in Front Loop Only of each sc across: 170 Ldc.

Row 4: Ch 1, turn; sc in Front Loop Only of each Ldc across.

Repeat Rows 3 and 4 for pattern until Afghan measures approximately 50" (127 cm) from beginning, ending by working Row 4.

Finish off.

Design by Kim Kotary.

WONDEROUS WHEELS

EASY

Finished Measurement:
Approx. 47" x 59" (119.5 cm x 150 cm)

MATERIALS

Deborah Norville Everyday™
Soft Worsted Solids (100% acrylic) MEDIUM 4
[4 ounces, 203 yards (114 grams, 185 meters) per skein]:
ED100-01 Snow White (MC) - 6 skeins
Deborah Norville Everyday™
Soft Worsted Prints (100% acrylic) MEDIUM 4
[3.5 ounces, 180 yards
(100 grams, 165 meters) per skein]:
ED200-04 Cotton Candy (CC1) - 3 skeins
ED200-06 Parrot (CC2) - 3 skeins
Crochet hook, size I (5.5 mm) **or** size needed for gauge
Yarn needle

GAUGE: Medium Motif = 7" (17.75 cm) diameter
Large Motif = 8½" (21.5 cm) diameter

Gauge Swatch: 5½" (14 cm) diameter
Work same as First Motif of Small Motif through Rnd 5.

STITCH GUIDE

FRONT POST TREBLE CROCHET *(abbreviated FPtr)*
YO twice, insert hook from **front** to **back** around post of st indicated *(Fig. 4, page 39)*, YO and pull up a loop (4 loops on hook), (YO and draw through 2 loops on hook) 3 times.

SMALL MOTIF

Make 10 with MC & CC1 and 10 with MC & CC2.

FIRST MOTIF

With MC, ch 4; join with slip st to form a ring.

Rnd 1 (Right side)**:** Ch 4 **(counts as first dc plus ch 1)**, (dc in ring, ch 1) 11 times, drop MC, carry unused color on **wrong** side of Motif; with CC, join with slip st to first dc ***(Fig. 3c, page 39)***: 12 dc and 12 ch-1 sps.

Rnd 2: Slip st in next ch-1 sp, ch 3 **(counts as first dc, now and throughout)**, 2 dc in same sp, 3 dc in each ch-1 sp around, drop CC; with MC, join with slip st to first dc: 36 dc.

Rnd 3: Ch 1, sc in same st, ch 3, skip next dc, sc in next dc, work FPtr around next dc 2 rows **below**, ★ sc in next dc, ch 3, skip next dc, sc in next dc, work FPtr around next dc 2 rows **below**; repeat from ★ around, drop MC; with CC, join with slip st to first sc: 36 sts and 12 ch-3 sps.

Rnd 4: (Slip st, ch 3, 3 dc**)** in next ch-3 sp, 4 dc in each ch-3 sp around, cut CC; with MC, join with slip st to first dc: 48 dc.

Rnd 5: Ch 1, sc in same st, ch 4, skip next 2 dc, sc in next dc, work FPtr around next FPtr 2 rows **below**, ★ sc in next dc, ch 4, skip next 2 dc, sc in next dc, work FPtr around next FPtr 2 rows **below**; repeat from ★ around; join with slip st to first sc, finish off: 36 sts and 12 ch-4 sps.

Instructions continued on page 16.

ADDITIONAL MOTIFS

Rnds 1-4: Work same as First Motif: 48 dc.

Referring to Placement Diagram, determine the number of joinings that will be necessary for this Motif. Small Motifs are joined to each previous Motif at 1 or 2 points. In some cases, it may be necessary for new Motifs to be joined in previous joinings.

Rnd 5 (Joining rnd)**:** Ch 1, sc in same st, ★ ch 2, with **right** side facing, slip st in ch-sp of **previous** Motif, ch 2, skip next 2 dc on **new** Motif, sc in next dc, work FPtr around next FPtr 2 rows **below**, sc in next dc; repeat from ★ as many times as necessary, ch 4, skip next 2 dc, sc in next dc, work FPtr around next FPtr 2 rows **below**, **(**sc in next dc, ch 4, skip next 2 dc, sc in next dc, work FPtr around next FPtr 2 rows **below)** around; join with slip st to first sc, finish off.

PLACEMENT DIAGRAM

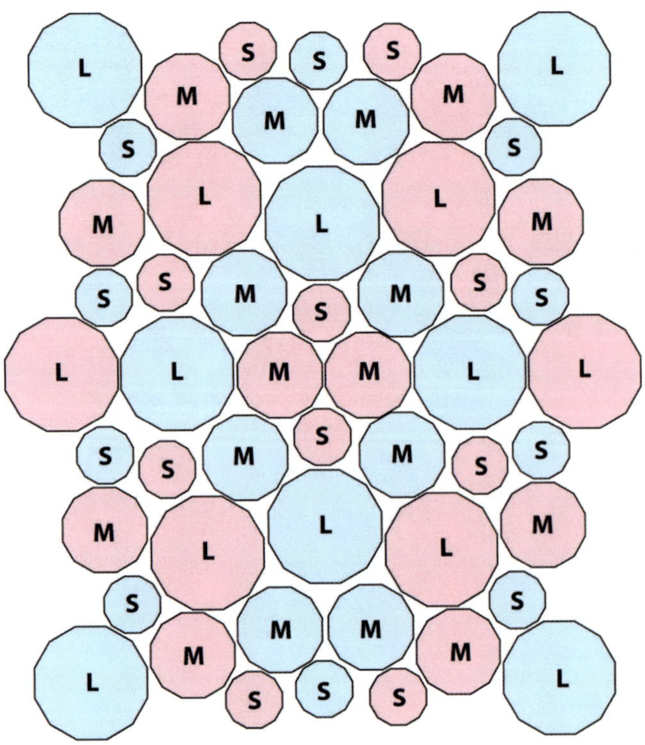

MEDIUM MOTIF

Make 10 with MC & CC1 and 8 with MC & CC2.

Rnds 1-4: Work same as First Motif of Small Motif; do **not** cut CC: 48 dc.

Rnd 5: Ch 1, sc in same st, ch 4, skip next 2 dc, sc in next dc, work FPtr around next FPtr 2 rows **below**, ★ sc in next dc, ch 4, skip next 2 dc, sc in next dc, work FPtr around next FPtr 2 rows **below**; repeat from ★ around, drop MC; with CC, join with slip st to first sc: 36 sts and 12 ch-4 sps.

Rnd 6: **(**Slip st, ch 3, 4 dc**)** in next ch-3 sp, 5 dc in each ch-3 sp around, cut CC; with MC, join with slip st to first dc: 60 dc.

Referring to Placement Diagram, determine the number of joinings that will be necessary for this Motif. Medium Motifs are joined to each previous Motif at 2 points. In some cases, it may be necessary for new Motifs to be joined in previous joinings.

Rnd 7 (Joining rnd)**:** Ch 1, sc in same st, ★ ch 2, with **right** side facing, slip st in ch-sp of **previous** Motif, ch 3, skip next 3 dc on **new** Motif, sc in next dc, work FPtr around next FPtr 2 rows **below**, sc in next dc; repeat from ★ as many times as necessary, ch 5, skip next 3 dc, sc in next dc, work FPtr around next FPtr 2 rows **below**, **(**sc in next dc, ch 5, skip next 3 dc, sc in next dc, work FPtr around next FPtr 2 rows **below)** around; join with slip st to first sc, finish off.

COLOR KEY

- MC & CC1 (pink)
- MC & CC2 (blue)

LARGE MOTIF

Make 6 with MC & CC1 and 8 with MC & CC2.

Rnds 1-4: Work same as First Motif of Small Motif; do **not** cut CC: 48 dc.

Rnd 5: Ch 1, sc in same st, ch 4, skip next 2 dc, sc in next dc, work FPtr around next FPtr 2 rows **below**, ★ sc in next dc, ch 4, skip next 2 dc, sc in next dc, work FPtr around next FPtr 2 rows **below**; repeat from ★ around, drop MC; with CC, join with slip st to first sc: 36 sts and 12 ch-4 sps.

Rnd 6: **(**Slip st, ch 3, 4 dc**)** in next ch-3 sp, 5 dc in each ch-3 sp around, drop CC; with MC, join with slip st to first dc: 60 dc.

Rnd 7: Ch 1, sc in same st, ch 5, skip next 3 dc, sc in next dc, work FPtr around next FPtr 2 rows **below**, ★ sc in next dc, ch 5, skip next 3 dc, sc in next dc, work FPtr around next FPtr 2 rows **below**; repeat from ★ around, drop MC; with CC, join with slip st to first sc: 36 sts and 12 ch-5 sps.

Rnd 8: **(**Slip st, ch 3, 5 dc**)** in next ch-3 sp, 6 dc in each ch-3 sp around, cut CC; with MC, join with slip st to first dc: 72 dc.

Referring to Placement Diagram, determine the number of joinings that will be necessary for this Motif. Large Motifs are joined to each previous Motif at 2 or 3 points. In some cases, it may be necessary for new Motifs to be joined in previous joinings.

Rnd 9 (Joining rnd)**:** Ch 1, sc in same st, ★ ch 3, with **right** side facing, slip st in ch-sp of **previous** Motif, ch 3, skip next 4 dc on **new** Motif, sc in next dc, work FPtr around next FPtr 2 rows **below**, sc in next dc; repeat from ★ as many times as necessary, ch 6, skip next 4 dc, sc in next dc, work FPtr around next FPtr 2 rows **below**, **(**sc in next dc, ch 6, skip next 4 dc, sc in next dc, work FPtr around next FPtr 2 rows **below)** around; join with slip st to first sc, finish off.

Design by Kim Kotary. ●

GREAT GRANNY! EASY

Finished Measurement:
Approx. 42" x 43" (106.5 cm x 109 cm)

MATERIALS
Deborah Norville Everyday™ Soft Worsted Prints (100% acrylic) MEDIUM 4
[3.5 ounces, 180 yards (100 grams, 165 meters) per skein]:
ED200-08 Parfait - 9 skeins
Deborah Norville Everyday™ Soft Worsted Solids (100% acrylic) MEDIUM 4
[4 ounces, 203 yards (114 grams, 185 meters)per skein]:
ED100-12 Black - 3 skeins
Crochet hook, size I (5.5 mm) **or** size needed for gauge
Yarn needle

GAUGE SWATCH: 5½" wide x 8" high (14 cm x 20.5 cm)
Work same as First Rectangle through Rnd 5.

STITCH GUIDE

TREBLE CROCHET *(abbreviated tr)* (uses one st)
YO twice, insert hook in st indicated, YO and pull up a loop (4 loops on hook), (YO and draw through 2 loops on hook) 3 times.

PICOT
Ch 3, slip st in top of last sc made.

JOINING PICOT
Ch 1, remove hook from loop, insert hook in corresponding Picot on **previous** Rectangle, pick up loop and pull loop through Picot, ch 1, slip st in top of last sc made on **new** Rectangle.

FIRST RECTANGLE

Foundation: With Parfait, (ch 4, tr in fourth ch from hook) 4 times: 4 loops.

Rnd 1 (Right side): Ch 3 **(counts as first dc, now and throughout)**, (2 dc, ch 2, 3 dc) in first loop (first corner), 3 dc in each of next 2 loops, 3 dc in last loop, (ch 2, 3 dc in same loop) twice (second and third corners); working on opposite side of loops, 3 dc in each of next 3 loops, ch 2 (fourth corner); join with slip st to first dc: 30 dc and 4 ch-2 sps.

Note: Loop a short piece of yarn around any stitch to mark Rnd 1 as **right** side.

Rnd 2: Slip st in next 2 dc and in next corner ch-2 sp, ch 3, (2 dc, ch 2, 3 dc) in same sp, [skip next 3 dc, 3 dc in sp **before** next dc *(Fig. 5, page 40)*] 3 times, (3 dc, ch 2, 3 dc) in each of next 2 corner ch-2 sps, (skip next 3 dc, 3 dc in sp **before** next dc) 3 times, (3 dc, ch 2, 3 dc) in last corner ch-2 sp; join with slip st to first dc: 42 dc and 4 ch-2 sps.

Rnds 3-5: Slip st in next 2 dc and in next corner ch-2 sp, ch 3, (2 dc, ch 2, 3 dc) in same sp, ★ (skip next 3 dc, 3 dc in sp **before** next dc) across to next corner ch-2 sp, (3 dc, ch 2, 3 dc) in corner ch-2 sp; repeat from ★ 2 times **more**, (skip next 3 dc, 3 dc in sp **before** next dc) across; join with slip st to first dc: 78 dc and 4 ch-2 sps.

Finish off.

EDGING

With **right** side facing, join Black with slip st in any corner ch-2 sp; ch 1, (2 sc in same sp, work Picot) twice, (sc in next 3 dc, work Picot) across to next corner ch-2 sp, ★ (2 sc, work Picot) twice in corner ch-2 sp, (sc in next 3 dc, work Picot) across to next corner ch-2 sp; repeat from ★ around; join with slip st to first sc, finish off.

ADDITIONAL RECTANGLES

Work same as First Rectangle through Rnd 5, then work One or Two Side Joining, referring to Placement Diagram for position and remembering that joined side will be the last one or two sides worked: 78 dc and 4 ch-2 sps.

ONE SIDE JOINING

With **right** side facing, join Black with slip st in corner ch-2 sp; ch 1, 2 sc in same sp, work Picot, (sc in next 3 dc, work Picot) across to next corner ch-2 sp, ★ (2 sc, work Picot) twice in corner ch-2 sp, (sc in next 3 dc, work Picot) across to next corner ch-2 sp; repeat from ★ once **more**, (2 sc, work Joining Picot) twice in corner ch-2 sp, (sc in next 3 dc, work Joining Picot) across to next corner ch-2 sp, 2 sc in same corner sp as first sc, work Joining Picot; join with slip st to first sc, finish off.

TWO SIDE JOINING

With **right** side facing, join Black with slip st in corner ch-2 sp; ch 1, 2 sc in same sp, work Picot, (sc in next 3 dc, work Picot) across to next corner ch-2 sp, (2 sc, work Picot) twice in corner ch-2 sp, (sc in next 3 dc, work Picot) across to next corner ch-2 sp, ★ (2 sc, work Joining Picot) twice in corner ch-2 sp, (sc in next 3 dc, work Joining Picot) across to next corner ch-2 sp; repeat from ★ once **more**, 2 sc in same corner sp as first sc, work Joining Picot; join with slip st to first sc, finish off.

PLACEMENT DIAGRAM

35	34	33	32	31	30	29
28	27	26	25	24	23	22
21	20	19	18	17	16	15
14	13	12	11	10	9	8
7	6	5	4	3	2	1

Design by Kim Kotary.

RUGGED **RIBS** EASY

Finished Measurement: Approx. 50" (127 cm) square

MATERIALS

Deborah Norville Everyday™ Soft Worsted Prints (100% acrylic) MEDIUM 4
[3.5 ounces, 180 yards (100 grams, 165 meters) per skein]:
ED200-11 Toasted Marshmallow - 16 skeins
Crochet hook, size K (6.5 mm) **or** size needed for gauge
Yarn needle

GAUGE: In pattern, 15 sts = 4½" (11.5 cm)
and 10 rows = 4" (10 cm)

Gauge Swatch: 5" wide x 4" high (12.75 cm x 10 cm)
Ch 19.
Work Rows 1-10 of Throw: 17 sts.
Finish off.

STITCH GUIDE

FRONT POST DOUBLE CROCHET *(abbreviated FPdc)*
YO, insert hook from **front** to **back** around post of st indicated *(Fig. 4, page 39)*, YO and pull up a loop (3 loops on hook), (YO and draw through 2 loops on hook) twice.

BACK POST DOUBLE CROCHET *(abbreviated BPdc)*
YO, insert hook from **back** to **front** around post of st indicated *(Fig. 4, page 39)*, YO and pull up a loop (3 loops on hook), (YO and draw through 2 loops on hook) twice.

THROW

Ch 169.

Row 1: Dc in fourth ch from hook **(3 skipped chs count as first dc)** and in each ch across: 167 dc.

Row 2 (Right side)**:** Ch 2, turn; hdc in first dc, work FPdc around each of next 5 dc, ★ work BPdc around each of next 5 dc, work FPdc around each of next 5 dc; repeat from ★ across to last dc, hdc in last dc.

Note: Loop a short piece of yarn around any stitch to mark Row 2 as **right** side.

Row 3: Ch 2, turn; hdc in first hdc, work BPdc around each of next 5 sts, ★ work FPdc around each of next 5 sts, work BPdc around each of next 5 sts; repeat from ★ across to last hdc, hdc in last hdc.

Row 4: Ch 2, hdc in first hdc, work FPdc around each of next 5 sts, ★ work BPdc around each of next 5 sts, work FPdc around each of next 5 sts; repeat from ★ across to last hdc, hdc in last hdc.

Repeat Rows 3 and 4 for pattern until Throw measures approximately 50" (127 cm) from beginning ch, ending by working Row 3.

Finish off.

Design by Vicki Blizzard. ●

SPANISH **LACE** EASY

Finished Measurement:

Approx. 48" x 52" (122 cm x 132 cm)

MATERIALS

Deborah Norville Everyday™
Soft Worsted Solids (100% acrylic) MEDIUM 4
[4 ounces, 203 yards (114 grams, 185 meters) per skein]:
ED100-07 Really Red - 10 skeins
Crochet hook, size I (5.5 mm) **or** size needed for gauge
Yarn needle

GAUGE: In pattern, one repeat = 2³/₄" wide (7 cm)
and 6 rows = 3" high (7.5 cm)

Gauge Swatch: 6" wide x 3³/₄" high (15.25 cm x 9.5 cm)
Ch 23.
Work Rows 1-7 of Afghan: 21 dc.
Finish off.

STITCH GUIDE

TREBLE CROCHET *(abbreviated tr)* (uses one st or sp)
YO twice, insert hook in st or sp indicated, YO and pull up a loop (4 loops on hook), (YO and draw through 2 loops on hook) 3 times.

CLUSTER (uses one sp)
YO twice, insert hook in sp indicated, YO and pull up a loop, (YO and draw through 2 loops on hook) twice, YO twice, insert hook in **same** sp, YO and pull up a loop, (YO and draw through 2 loops on hook) twice, YO and draw through all 3 loops on hook.

AFGHAN

Ch 191.

Row 1 (Right side): Dc in fourth ch from hook **(3 skipped chs count as first dc)** and in each ch across: 189 dc.

Note: Loop a short piece of yarn around any stitch to mark Row 1 as **right** side.

Row 2: Ch 1, turn; sc in first 2 dc, ch 3, ★ skip next 2 dc, sc in next dc, ch 3; repeat from ★ across to last 4 dc, skip next 2 dc, sc in last 2 dc: 65 sc and 62 ch-3 sps.

Row 3: Ch 1, turn; sc in first 2 sc, ch 1, sc in next ch-3 sp, (ch 3, sc in next ch-3 sp) across to last 2 sc, ch 1, sc in last 2 sc: 66 sc and 63 sps.

Row 4: Ch 4 **(counts as first dc plus ch 1)**, turn; (2 dc in next sp, ch 1) across to last 2 sc, skip next sc, dc in last sc: 128 dc and 64 ch-1 sps.

Row 5: Ch 1, turn; sc in first dc and in next ch-1 sp, ch 1, skip next ch-1 sp and next dc, (work Cluster, ch 1) 3 times in sp **before** next dc ***(Fig. 5, page 40)***, skip next ch-1 sp, sc in next ch-1 sp, ★ ch 3, sc in next ch-1 sp, ch 1, skip next ch-1 sp and next dc, (work Cluster, ch 1) 3 times in sp **before** next dc, skip next ch-1 sp, sc in next ch-1 sp; repeat from ★ across to last dc, sc in last dc: 48 Clusters, 34 sc, and 79 sps.

Row 6: Ch 4 **(counts as first tr)**, turn; tr in next sc, ch 1, skip next ch-1 sp, sc in next ch-1 sp, ch 3, sc in next ch-1 sp, ★ ch 3, skip next ch-1 sp, (tr, ch 3) twice in next ch-3 sp, skip next ch-1 sp, sc in next ch-1 sp, ch 3, sc in next ch-1 sp; repeat from ★ across to last ch-1 sp, ch 1, skip last ch-1 sp, tr in last 2 sc: 66 sts and 63 sps.

Row 7: Ch 3 **(counts as first dc)**, turn; dc in next tr and in next ch-1 sp, 3 dc in each ch-3 sp across to last ch-1 sp, dc in last ch-1 sp and in last 2 tr: 189 dc.

Repeat Rows 2-7 for pattern until Afghan measures approximately 50" (127 cm) from beginning ch, ending by working Row 7; do **not** finish off.

EDGING

Ch 4 **(counts as first tr)**; working in end of rows, 8 tr in end of first row, (skip next 2 rows, sc in next row, skip next 2 rows, 9 tr in next row) across to next corner; working **between** dc on Row 1, skip first 5 dc, sc in sp **before** next dc, (skip next 6 dc, 9 tr in sp **before** next dc, skip next 6 dc, sc in sp **before** next dc) across to last 4 dc, skip last 4 dc; working in end of rows, 9 tr in end of first row, (skip next 2 rows, sc in next row, skip next 2 rows, 9 tr in next row) across to next corner; working across last row, skip first 4 dc, sc in next dc, (skip next 5 dc, 9 tr in next dc, skip next 5 dc, sc in next dc) across to last 4 dc, skip last 4 dc; join with slip st to first tr, finish off.

Design by Lisa Gentry.

BEST FRIENDS: **HIPPO & RHINO** EASY

HIPPO

Finished Measurement:
Approx. 11" long x 8" high (28 cm x 20.5 cm)

MATERIALS
Deborah Norville Everyday™ Soft Worsted Prints (100% acrylic) MEDIUM 4
[3.5 ounces, 180 yards
(100 grams, 165 meters) per skein]:
ED200-05 Lagoon - 2 skeins
Deborah Norville Everyday™ Soft Worsted Solids (100% acrylic) MEDIUM 4
[4 ounces, 203 yards (114 grams, 185 meters) per skein]:
ED100-12 Black - small amount
Crochet hook size G (4 mm) **or** size needed for gauge
Polyester stuffing
9 mm black animal eyes - 2
Yarn needle

Note: If toy is intended for children under 3 years old, we recommend embroidering the eyes.

GAUGE: 8 sc and 9 rows = 2" (5 cm)

Gauge Swatch: 2" (5 cm) square
Row 1: Ch 9; sc in second ch from hook and in each ch across: 8 sc.
Rows 2-9: Ch 1, turn; sc in each sc across.
Finish off.

STITCH GUIDE

DECREASE
Pull up a loop in each of next 2 sc, YO and draw through all 3 loops on hook **(counts as one sc)**.

HEAD

With Lagoon and beginning at snout, ch 10.

Rnd 1 (Right side)**:** Sc in second ch from hook and in next 7 chs, 3 sc in last ch; working in free loops of beginning ch *(Fig. 2b, page 39)*, sc in next 7 chs, 2 sc in next ch; do **not** join, place marker *(see Markers, page 39)*: 20 sc.

Rnd 2: 2 Sc in next sc, sc in next 7 sc, 2 sc in each of next 3 sc, sc in next 7 sc, 2 sc in each of next 2 sc: 26 sc.

Rnd 3: (Sc in next 5 sc, 2 sc in next sc) 4 times, sc in next 2 sc: 30 sc.

Rnd 4: (Sc in next 4 sc, 2 sc in next sc) around: 36 sc.

Rnds 5-15: Sc in each sc around.

Rnd 16: (Sc in next 4 sc, decrease) around: 30 sc.

Rnds 17-21: Sc in each sc around.

Rnd 22: (Sc in next 3 sc, decrease) around: 24 sc.

Attach eyes between Rnds 15 and 16 on top of Head, leaving 4 sts between eyes.

Rnd 23: Sc in each sc around.

Stuff Head.

Rnd 24: (Sc in next 2 sc, decrease) around: 18 sc.

Rnd 25: (Sc in next sc, decrease) around: 12 sc.

Rnd 26: Decrease around; finish off leaving a 6" (15 cm) end for sewing: 6 sc.

Thread yarn needle with end and weave through remaining sts; pull **tightly** to close and secure end.

BODY

Rnd 1 (Right side)**:** With Lagoon, ch 2; 6 sc in second ch from hook; do **not** join, place marker.

Rnd 2: 2 Sc in each sc around: 12 sc.

Rnd 3: (Sc in next sc, 2 sc in next sc) around: 18 sc.

Rnd 4: (Sc in next 2 sc, 2 sc in next sc) around: 24 sc.

Rnd 5: (Sc in next 3 sc, 2 sc in next sc) around: 30 sc.

Rnd 6: (Sc in next 4 sc, 2 sc in next sc) around: 36 sc.

Rnd 7: (Sc in next 5 sc, 2 sc in next sc) around: 42 sc.

Rnd 8: Sc in each sc around.

Rnd 9: (Sc in next 6 sc, 2 sc in next sc) around: 48 sc.

Rnd 10: (Sc in next 7 sc, 2 sc in next sc) around: 54 sc.

Rnd 11: Sc in each sc around.

Rnd 12: (Sc in next 8 sc, 2 sc in next sc) around: 60 sc.

Rnds 13-30: Sc in each sc around.

Rnd 31: (Sc in next 8 sc, decrease) around: 54 sc.

Rnd 32: Sc in each sc around.

Rnd 33: (Sc in next 7 sc, decrease) around: 48 sc.

Rnd 34: Sc in each sc around.

Rnd 35: (Sc in next 6 sc, decrease) around: 42 sc.

Rnd 36: (Sc in next 5 sc, decrease) around: 36 sc.

Rnd 37: (Sc in next 4 sc, decrease) around: 30 sc.

Rnd 38: (Sc in next 3 sc, decrease) around: 24 sc.

Rnd 39: (Sc in next 2 sc, decrease) around: 18 sc.

Stuff Body.

Rnd 40: (Sc in next sc, decrease) around: 12 sc.

Rnd 41: Decrease around; finish off leaving a 6" (15 cm) end for sewing: 6 sc.

Thread yarn needle with end and weave through remaining sts; pull **tightly** to close and secure end.

LEG (Make 4)

Rnd 1 (Right side)**:** With Lagoon, ch 2; 6 sc in second ch from hook; do **not** join, place marker.

Rnd 2: 2 Sc in each sc around: 12 sc.

Rnd 3: (Sc in next sc, 2 sc in next sc) around: 18 sc.

Rnd 4: (Sc in next 2 sc, 2 sc in next sc) around: 24 sc.

Rnd 5: Working in Front Loops Only ***(Fig. 1, page 39)***, (sc in next 3 sc, 2 sc in next sc) around: 30 sc.

Rnd 6: Ch 1, working in free loops of Rnd 4 ***(Fig. 2a, page 39)***, sc in each sc around: 24 sc.

Rnds 7-13: Sc in both loops of each sc around; at end of Rnd 13, finish off leaving a 10" (25.5 cm) end for sewing: 24 sc.

Stuff Leg and sew to Body.

Instructions continued on page 33.

WORKING IN A SPACE BEFORE A STITCH

When instructed to work in a space before a stitch or in spaces between stitches, insert hook in space indicated by arrow *(Fig. 5)*.

Fig. 5

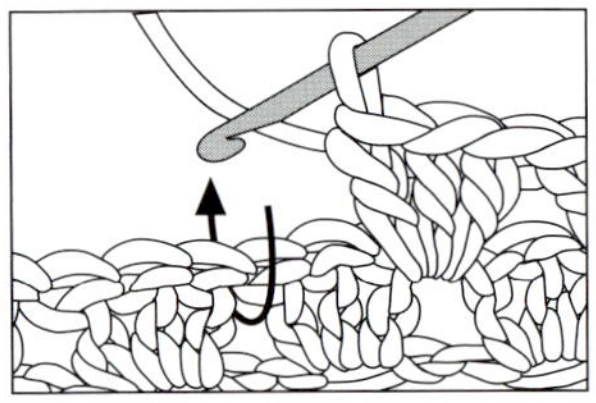

WHIPSTITCH

With **wrong** sides together, sew through both pieces once to secure the beginning of the seam, leaving an ample yarn end to weave in later. Insert the needle from **front** to **back** through **both** loops on **both** pieces *(Fig. 6)*. Bring the needle around and insert it from **front** to **back** through next loops of both pieces. Continue across in this manner, keeping the sewing yarn fairly loose.

Fig. 6

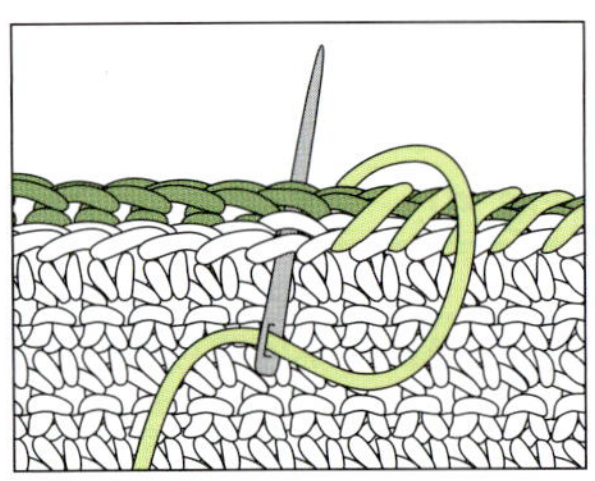

SATIN STITCH

Satin stitch is a series of straight stitches worked side-by-side so they touch but do not overlap. Come up at odd numbers and go down at even numbers *(Fig. 7)*.

Fig. 7

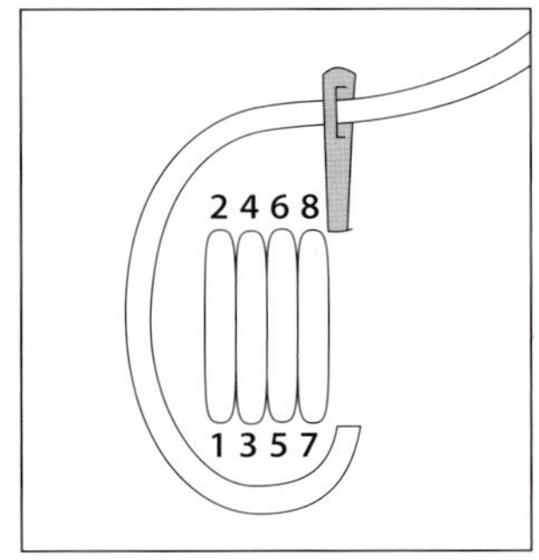

STRAIGHT STITCH

Straight stitch is just what the name implies, a single, straight stitch. Come up at 1 and go down at 2 *(Fig. 8)*.

Fig. 8

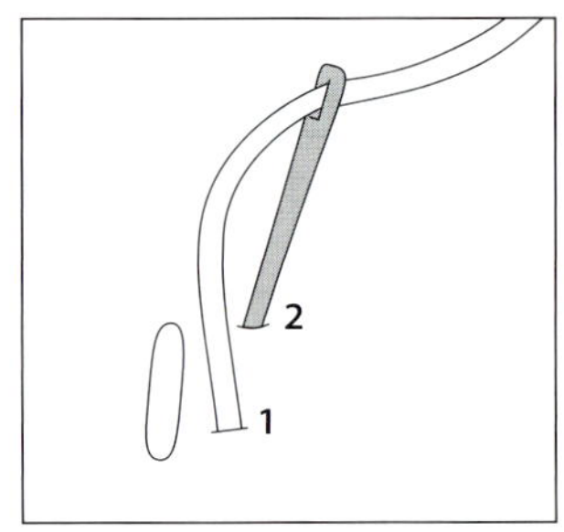

Production Team: Writers/Technical Editors - Joan Beebe and Linda A. Daley; Editorial Writer - Susan McManus Johnson; Senior Graphic Artist - Lora Puls; Graphic Artist - Becca Snider; Photo Stylists - Sondra Daniel and Cora Holdaway; and Photographers - Jason Masters and Ken West.

Rnd 7: (Sc in next 5 sc, 2 sc in next sc) around: 42 sc.

Rnd 8: Sc in each sc around.

Rnd 9: (Sc in next 6 sc, 2 sc in next sc) around: 48 sc.

Rnd 10: (Sc in next 7 sc, 2 sc in next sc) around: 54 sc.

Rnd 11: Sc in each sc around.

Rnd 12: (Sc in next 8 sc, 2 sc in next sc) around: 60 sc.

Rnds 13-30: Sc in each sc around.

Rnd 31: (Sc in next 8 sc, decrease) around: 54 sc.

Rnd 32: Sc in each sc around.

Rnd 33: (Sc in next 7 sc, decrease) around: 48 sc.

Rnd 34: Sc in each sc around.

Rnd 35: (Sc in next 6 sc, decrease) around: 42 sc.

Rnd 36: (Sc in next 5 sc, decrease) around: 36 sc.

Rnd 37: (Sc in next 4 sc, decrease) around: 30 sc.

Rnd 38: (Sc in next 3 sc, decrease) around: 24 sc.

Rnd 39: (Sc in next 2 sc, decrease) around: 18 sc.

Stuff Body.

Rnd 40: (Sc in next sc, decrease) around: 12 sc.

Rnd 41: Decrease around; finish off leaving a 6" (15 cm) end for sewing: 6 sc.

Thread yarn needle with end and weave through remaining sts; pull **tightly** to close and secure end.

LEG (Make 4)

Rnd 1 (Right side)**:** With Lagoon, ch 2; 6 sc in second ch from hook; do **not** join, place marker.

Rnd 2: 2 Sc in each sc around: 12 sc.

Rnd 3: (Sc in next sc, 2 sc in next sc) around: 18 sc.

Rnd 4: (Sc in next 2 sc, 2 sc in next sc) around: 24 sc.

Rnd 5: Working in Front Loops Only ***(Fig. 1, page 39)***, (sc in next 3 sc, 2 sc in next sc) around: 30 sc.

Rnd 6: Ch 1, working in free loops of Rnd 4 ***(Fig. 2a, page 39)***, sc in each sc around: 24 sc.

Rnds 7-13: Sc in both loops of each sc around; at end of Rnd 13, finish off leaving a 10" (25.5 cm) end for sewing: 24 sc.

Stuff Leg and sew to Body.

Instructions continued on page 33.

CAT NAP **PILLOW**

EASY

Approximate Finished Measurements:

21" long (53.5 cm) from tip of Tail to top of Head
$17^1/_2$" wide (44.5 cm) from ends of Back Legs
Pillow Body measures 15" wide x 13" high (38 cm x 33 cm) (before stuffing)

MATERIALS

Deborah Norville Everyday™ Soft Worsted Prints (100% acrylic) [3.5 ounces, 180 yards (100 grams, 165 meters) per skein]:
 #200-06 Parrot - 4 skeins

MEDIUM 4

Deborah Norville Everyday™ Soft Worsted Solids (100% acrylic) [4 ounces, 203 yards (114 grams, 185 meters) per skein]:
 #100-12 Black - small amount

MEDIUM 4

Crochet hook size H (5 mm) **or** size needed for gauge
Polyester stuffing
12 mm buttons for eyes - 2
1" (25 mm) button for Tab - 1
Yarn needle

Note: If toy is intended for children under 3 years old, we recommend embroidering the eyes.

GAUGE: 7 sc and 8 rows = 2" (5 cm)

Gauge Swatch: 2" (5 cm) square
Ch 8.
Work same as Pillow Body Rows 1-8: 7 sc.
Finish off.

STITCH GUIDE

DECREASE
Pull up a loop in each of next 2 sc, YO and draw through all 3 loops on hook **(counts as one sc)**.

PILLOW BODY (Make 2)

With Parrot, ch 55.

Row 1 (Right side)**:** Sc in second ch from hook and each ch across: 54 sc.

Note: Loop a short piece of yarn around any stitch to mark Row 1 as **right** side.

Rows 2-52: Ch 1, turn; sc in each sc across; at end of Row 52, finish off.

With **right** sides together and sts and rows matching, sew both pieces together, stuffing Pillow Body lightly before closing.

HEAD

Row 1: With Parrot, ch 2; 6 sc in second ch from hook.

Row 2 (Right side)**:** Ch 1, turn; 2 sc in each sc across: 12 sc.

Note: Mark Row 2 as **right** side.

Row 3: Ch 1, turn; sc in first sc, 2 sc in next sc, (sc in next sc, 2 sc in next sc) across: 18 sc.

Row 4: Ch 1, turn; sc in first 2 sc, 2 sc in next sc, (sc in next 2 sc, 2 sc in next sc) across: 24 sc.

Row 5: Ch 1, turn; sc in first 3 sc, 2 sc in next sc, (sc in next 3 sc, 2 sc in next sc) across: 30 sc.

Row 6: Ch 1, turn; sc in each sc across.

Row 7: Ch 1, turn; sc in first 4 sc, 2 sc in next sc, (sc in next 4 sc, 2 sc in next sc) across: 36 sc.

Row 8: Ch 1, turn; sc in each sc across.

Row 9: Ch 1, turn; sc in first 5 sc, 2 sc in next sc, (sc in next 5 sc, 2 sc in next sc) across: 42 sc.

Row 10: Ch 1, turn; sc in each sc across.

Row 11: Ch 1, turn; sc in first 6 sc, 2 sc in next sc, (sc in next 6 sc, 2 sc in next sc) across: 48 sc.

Rows 12-20: Ch 1, turn; sc in each sc across.

Row 21: Ch 1, turn; sc in first 6 sc, decrease, (sc in next 6 sc, decrease) across: 42 sc.

Row 22: Ch 1, turn; sc in first 5 sc, decrease, (sc in next 5 sc, decrease) across: 36 sc.

Row 23: Ch 1, turn; sc in first 4 sc, decrease, (sc in next 4 sc, decrease) across: 30 sc.

Row 24: Ch 1, turn; sc in each sc across; finish off.

Sew end of rows together; stuff Head lightly. Center Head on one long side of Pillow Body and sew in place, adding more stuffing if needed before closing.

EAR (Make 2)

Row 1 (Right side)**:** With Parrot ch 2; 6 sc in second ch from hook.

Note: Mark Row 1 as **right** side.

Row 2: Ch 1, turn; sc in each sc across.

Row 3: Ch 1, turn; sc in first sc, 2 sc in next sc, (sc in next sc, 2 sc in next sc) across: 9 sc.

Row 4: Ch 1, turn; sc in each sc across.

Row 5: Ch 1, turn; sc in first 2 sc, 2 sc in next sc, (sc in next 2 sc, 2 sc in next sc) across: 12 sc.

Row 6: Ch 1, turn; sc in each sc across.

Row 7: Ch 1, turn; sc in first 3 sc, 2 sc in next sc, (sc in next 3 sc, 2 sc in next sc) across: 15 sc.

Instructions continued on page 34.

A REAL **HOOT**

EASY

Finished Measurement:
Approx. 6" wide x 10" high (15 cm x 25.5 cm)

MATERIALS

Deborah Norville Everyday™
Soft Worsted Prints (100% acrylic) MEDIUM 4
[3.5 ounces, 180 yards
(100 grams, 165 meters) per skein]:
ED200-12 Flashback - 1 skein
Deborah Norville Everyday™
Soft Worsted Solids (100% acrylic) MEDIUM 4
[4 ounces, 203 yards (114 grams, 185 meters) per skein]:
ED100-07 Really Red - 1 skein
ED100-01 White - 1 skein
ED100-12 Black - 1 skein
Crochet hook, size G (4 mm) **or** size needed for gauge
Polyester stuffing
Yarn needle

GAUGE: 8 sc and 9 rows = 2" (5 cm)

Gauge Swatch: 2" (5 cm) square
Row 1: Ch 9; sc in second ch from hook and in each ch across: 8 sc.
Rows 2-9: Ch 1, turn; sc in each sc across.
Finish off.

STITCH GUIDE

DECREASE
Pull up a loop in each of next 2 sc, YO and draw through all 3 loops on hook **(counts as one sc)**.

BODY

With Really Red and beginning at top of head, ch 9.

Rnd 1 (Right side)**:** 3 Sc in second ch from hook, sc in next 6 chs, 3 sc in last ch; working in free loops of beginning ch *(Fig. 2b, page 39)*, sc in next 6 chs; do **not** join, place marker *(see Markers, page 39)*: 18 sc.

Rnd 2: Sc in next sc, 3 sc in next sc, sc in next 8 sc, 3 sc in next sc, sc in each sc around: 22 sc.

Rnd 3: Sc in next 2 sc, 3 sc in next sc, sc in next 10 sc, 3 sc in next sc, sc in each sc around: 26 sc.

Rnd 4: Sc in next 3 sc, 3 sc in next sc, sc in next 12 sc, 3 sc in next sc, sc in each sc around: 30 sc.

Rnd 5: Sc in next 4 sc, 3 sc in next sc, sc in next 14 sc, 3 sc in next sc, sc in each sc around: 34 sc.

Rnd 6: Sc in next 5 sc, 3 sc in next sc, sc in next 16 sc, 3 sc in next sc, sc in each sc around: 38 sc.

Rnd 7: Sc in next 6 sc, 3 sc in next sc, sc in next 18 sc, 3 sc in next sc, sc in each sc around: 42 sc.

Rnd 8: Sc in next 7 sc, 3 sc in next sc, sc in next 20 sc, 3 sc in next sc, sc in each sc around: 46 sc.

Rnds 9-15: Sc in each sc around.

Rnd 16: Sc in next 4 sc, decrease, sc in next 5 sc, decrease, (sc in next 6 sc, decrease) twice, sc in next 5 sc, decrease, sc in next 6 sc, decrease, sc in next 2 sc: 40 sc.

Rnds 17-20: Sc in each sc around.

Rnd 21: (Sc in next 4 sc, 2 sc in next sc) around: 48 sc.

Rnds 22-48: Sc in each sc around; at end of Rnd 48, slip st in next sc and finish off.

RUFFLE FEATHERS

With Flashback, ch 42.

Row 1 (Right side)**:** Sc in second ch from hook and in each ch across: 41 sc.

Note: Loop a short piece of yarn around any stitch to mark Row 1 as **right** side.

Row 2: Ch 3 **(counts as first dc, now and throughout)**, turn; 3 dc in first sc, ★ skip next 2 sc, (sc, ch 2, 3 dc) in next sc; repeat from ★ across to last sc, sc in last sc: 57 sts and 13 ch-2 sps.